1

Table of Contents

Introduction

As a new mother, you have a million plates spinning all at once. You are worried about taking care of your child and all the responsibilities that come with this. On top of the full time childcare duties, you also need to worry about keeping up with friends, making supper, and keeping your husband and other family members happy. The last thing on your mind is decluttering your home and making it look nice. But this is an important thing and doing upkeep on your house each day can make it much more presentable once company comes knocking. With the helpful tips in this guidebook, you can spend just a few minutes on each task in order to get each room of the home cleaned up and looking great.

The first chapter starts out with the living room. As a new parent, you probably spend a lot of time in this room taking care of the baby, visiting with others, and just relaxing. This chapter talks about some of the best decluttering tips like throwing away the trash right away, using magazine stands, and having a toy box for those toys that never seem to go away. Once you are done with the living room, it is time to work on the kitchen. When you are done with a meal each day, it is easy to run to the living room to relax. But with some simple tips, like keeping up with the dishes and sweeping the floor, you will get your kitchen looking great in just a few minutes.

Next comes the bathroom. One issue with most homes is that the bathroom is small even though it holds a lot of items. Once a baby comes into the picture, the amount of items in the bathroom seems to multiply. This chapter will spend some time discussing ways to add more room to the bathroom while also making it safer for the new child. Having a bedroom that is clutter free and clean is important to getting some good sleep at night, especially when you are dealing with a baby. This chapter goes into the best ways to make your room a restful and clean sleep haven so you can wake up recharged and ready to take on the day.

Now that you have that new baby, it is important to keep their rooms as clean as possible. While you may have to work on their room while they are awake, eliciting lots of cries for attention, some of the tips in the chapter on baby's room can make it easier to clean up the room and making it look like no child lives in there. We next move on to the closet. While this chapter will discuss the hall closet where lots of coats and mismatched items end up, you can use these tips to help out with any closet in the house. This is an area of the home that often has lots of things throw in side to keep them out of the way which means you might have to spend some time getting the area clean.

Cleaning the toy room is a topic that can give any parent a headache. It always seems that as soon as you get the toys cleaned up, your baby is going to have them all out on the floor and in the way two seconds later. With the tips inside this chapter, you will be able to find quick ways to clean up the toys in just a few minutes. Now let's get to the storage room. This is another area where a lot of random items are thrown. Most mothers throw items down there assuming they will get back to the work later on. In reality, items just keep getting left down there until it becomes a mess. With the help of the tips in this chapter, you can clean up the storage room in no time and actually find everything you need.

It's time to discuss the one item that every mother needs to have on hand any time they go out in public. The diaper bag is your lifeline when leaving the home with a new baby and when it's stocked correctly, the trip can go much easier. This chapter is going to spend some time taking about how to keep the diaper bag updated with all the right storage so you can go out and about without a worry. Everyone has those friends and relatives who seem to forget you have a new child on your hand. They stop by whenever they feel like it, often waking the baby up in the process or announce they will be by in just a few short hours. Of course, they also expect the house to look amazing. The chapter on tidying up for company takes a bit of time to look at quick and easy decluttering tips that you can try out in order to make your home look like you spent all day cleaning it up.

The final chapter finishes out this guidebook with some tips to keep your vehicle cleaned up and ready for your child. You will spend a good amount of time in your vehicle whether you are just going out for some groceries or hitting the road to see some family. This time is not going to be much fun for you or the baby without the proper preparation. With this chapter, you will learn what things are good to bring along in the car no matter where you are going to have the best trip possible.

Decluttering and cleaning your home as a busy mom can seem almost impossible. With the help of the tips in this guidebook, you can get your home to look amazing and only spend a few minutes each day.

Decluttering Your Living Room

As a new mother, you probably spend a lot of time in the living room. This is where you hold baby, entertain guests, and probably fall asleep on the couch more than you are willing to admit. Since you spend so much time in this room, it is critical that you take care to keep rid of the clutter. But as a new mother, you also understand that time for cleaning and decluttering are limited while taking care a baby. Here are a few of the best tips that you can use in order to declutter your living room and make it look like you spent all day cleaning.

Tip #1: The magazines and books

While the baby is napping so peacefully on your chest, you may not be able to fall asleep. This is when your favorite magazine or book comes out and you get some quality time catching up with the latest gossip or romance. Once the baby wakes up, you might throw the magazine on the floor or table and forget all about it until the heap of old papers and magazines get in your way.

Cleaning up your magazines does not have to be a difficult task and with the right steps, you can even make it go in with your décor. One idea is to find some woven baskets, any color will do so have some fun, and leave them by the couch or in a magazine corner. You can leave all the magazines in there and grab them whenever you need a nice read. If you're not much of a magazine reader, this idea works well for those little items that get in the way but don't have their own place in the room.

Tip #2: Picture frames

It is fine to be proud of your family, especially those children that are your pride and joy and take up every minute of your life. But all those picture frames on the table and all over the place are making the living room look cluttered and they are likely to get broken as your child gets older. Instead of getting rid of the pictures though, just learn how to use them in a different way.

Many mothers choose to keep the picture frames but hang them on the wall. This works in several ways. First, you get to keep the pictures that you love so much. Second, the pictures are out of the way so you aren't bumping against them and causing a mess. Thirdly, your living room gets a brand new look thanks to these pictures being placed in a decorative way on the wall. One day when the baby is sleeping, get some sticky tape and organize the pictures on a wall you aren't using and see what a change it can make.

Tip #3: Shelves

Shelves can be your best fried as a mother. Even if you just throw things on them willy-nilly, it still makes the room look much better than leaving these items on the floor. You can pick up anything that is on the floor, including books, toys, magazines, and movies, and place them on these shelves.

Have some fun with this. Some people will be fine with a little corner shelf that can hold a few things while others might devote a whole wall to this project. Consider the amount of space that you have as well as the number of items you plan to put on these shelves to make the process easier.

Tip #4: Be armed with trash bags

When doing a decluttering project, make sure to come armed with at least one big sized garbage bag in hand. Many mothers start out with the best of intentions and spend the majority of their time running back and forth between the living room and their garbage can. This can waste a lot of time and soon the baby is back awake before you finished the task at hand.

So when you get started, keep a few garbage bags in tow. You can start clearing up the room by picking up all trash that you see and filling the garbage bag. If you're short on time, ignore all the other mess and just pick up the papers, cups, and other items that are not considered trash. Even though you missed some of the other mess, the room is going to look a lot better without all the trash piling up.

Tip #5: Work on the movies

As your child gets older, you are certain to have movies lying around no matter where you go. Their favorite characters are popping up in your dreams now and figuring out the best way to get things organized is important. These videos take up a lot of space. If you put in those shelves, save some room to place the DVD's on top. Another idea is a movie holder. This allows you to throw out the cases to all your movies and keep the discs in one area. The holder is small and light and you can place it up high to keep the DVD's free from sticky fingers.

Tip #6: Blankets

The living room is the major traffic area for being comfortable and cuddling up with some great blankets. When you are cuddling with a baby, having extra blankets around can make things even better. But when you look around the living room and see tons of blankets on the floor, it is easy to think your house has been taken over.

Instead of leaving the blankets on the floor or trying to hide them away in another location, it is a good idea to find a spot in the living room to hold these items. There are many storage containers that will work. Some mothers like to use an ottoman so it matches in with the furniture. Others might find a nice wooden chest that adds to the room but which can hold all the big blankets. Choose something that is functional and pretty to make the room look amazing.

Tip #7: Laundry

As a new mother, it is easy to leave clothes lying on the floor. You have to change the baby at least a few times each day when they get messy and the older kids are not often much easier. But after a few days, you have a big heap of clothes lying all of the floor that looks almost as bad as the trash you just picked up.

As you are cleaning, take five minutes to pick up the clothes lying on the floor. This will clear up a lot of space and give you some peace of mind. After this clean up session, make sure to leave a nice laundry basket nearby. You can just place it in a corner with the lid on. Any time you have a dirty outfit to dispose of, throw the item into the laundry basket to keep the floor looking clean.

Tip #8: Put dishes away

It might be a pain, but any time you are done eating in the living room, make sure to go put the dishes away as soon as possible. This ensures that the dishes are getting washed and that you aren't dealing with dirty dishes clouding up the living room. Any time that you clean up a living room, bring with you a little box. Throw the dishes in here all together and then take them back to the kitchen at the same time. This makes the process easier and saves a lot of trips.

Tip #9: Organize the toys

Whether you have one child or more, you are probably stepping on toys all day long. Right after you clean up the toys, they are all out on the floor two seconds later and this can be a pain. It is a good idea to find some methods to cleaning up the toys without pulling your hair out.

Most mothers choose to run back and forth with toys in their arms and throw the toys into their children's rooms. Another idea is to find a toy box or a little storage unit to keep in the living room that can be out of the way and hold everything. This prevents time wasted from running to the rooms and back, especially since the children will just bring the toys back out. If you must keep the toys in their rooms, grab a basket and place toys inside to cut down on the trips.

Tip #10: Vacuum

You might want to hold off on this one until the baby wakes up or when someone is home to help out since the vacuum makes a lot of noise, but it's still a good step to take. A room just doesn't feel clean without a quick vacuum to get things in place.

Move furniture around as much as you can and get under everything for a nice clean feeling.

These easy tips take just minutes each day to get done and when split up between naps and the few minutes to yourself, you can have a clean and organized living room for the whole family to enjoy.

Keeping the Kitchen Tidy

Once you are done cleaning out the living room, or on a different day, you should move on to the kitchen. This is a room that gets pretty messy as you prepare meals and snacks for the kids to enjoy and keeping it tidy can seem like a full time job. Here are some of the tips that you can use to get your kitchen looking shiny and nice in no time.

Tip #1: Toss it away

Kitchens can hold on to a lot of items that you might not even notice are there. You probably kept an item in the hopes of using them in the future, but in reality they get stuck in the back of your cabinets taking up space. Take everything out of your cabinets and look at them. Do they work? Are they yours? Have you actually used them in the past five years? If you never use them and they don't work, throw the item out. These just take up space and make your kitchen look like a mess. Also, if you have more than one of an item, unless you use them all the time, throw the older one out.

Tip #2: Replace what doesn't work

It is common for people to have items that don't even work in their kitchens. These are items they plan on using later but usually get stuffed in the back of a cabinet and never fixed. These items are now lying on your counter and you might not have used them for years. At this point, do not shove them back into the cabinet or cupboard. Instead, fix them right now or throw them out. You have most likely purchased a replacement or it will save you time to go and get one now. Save yourself the hassle and get a new item that works well and probably takes up less space.

Tip #3: Organize by use

Place the items that you use the most often in an area that is easy to get. You probably waste a lot of time reaching to the back of the cabinet or searching around for an item that you plan to use for a meal. It is often found behind a lot of other items that you rarely if ever use. This means it's time to reorganize the area so all of the things that you use on a regular basis are easy to find.

There are two ways that you can do this process. First, take all of the items that you don't use that often but which you plan to keep and place them in the back of the cupboard. This makes it easy for you to find the items when needed but keeps them out of the way for awhile. You can then place the items that are used more often in the front. Next time you go to open up a cupboard, the item you need is right there in the front.

Another option is to assign cupboards to your items. Pick out the ones that are at eye level or easy to find and place all your most used items in these cupboards. Place the items that you don't use as often in the bottom or harder to reach cupboards so they are out of the way but still reachable when needed. Now you can get to your most used items at any time and speed up supper.

Tip #4: Store by use

When you are making most of your meals, there are items that often go together. You might use the soup pot with the ladle and the skillet with another tool and the strainer. Instead of searching all over the kitchen for each of these items, it might be easier to place them together for easier access.

So while all the items are out, determine what items you commonly use together. Every person uses their kitchen slightly differently so you will not organize your kitchen in the same way that someone else does.

Tip #5: Keep up on dishes

Having just a few dishes out on the counter can make the whole place look like a mess. You need to keep up with the dishes as much as possible. While this might sound a bit impossible when you are dealing with little ones, you will find it is much easier to spend five minutes on the dishes rather than an hour or more later on.

The best way to go about this process is to wash the dishes after every use. When you are done with lunch, go through and clean up the dishes that you are using. When you have a snack, rinse off the silverware and plates before putting them away. If you're day gets really busy, at least take the time to clean up the dishes after supper before you head to bed.

Tip #6: Clean the counters

Once the dishes are finished, take the time to clean off the counters. While a cloth with warm water is a good place to start, you need to take it a step further and clean off the clutter. The kitchen counter can get a lot of clutter on top from paperwork to school supplies and other things that don't even belong there. Over time, this begins to make the kitchen look messy. So the first place you should start is cleaning off the counter.

Take a look at each object and determine if this is an item that even belongs in the kitchen. If the item doesn't belong in the kitchen, either go put it back in the correct spot or throw it out. For the other items, put them away in the drawers and cupboards. While a few items can remain on the counter if you are out of room or you use them often, most of the items on your counters have no place being there and can be removed.

When you are done with this process, you will see that the counter is cleared off of most items. You can now get some soap and water and clean off the counters until they shine. From now on, take the time to clean off the counter each day and give it a good scrub to make the kitchen look better.

Tip #7: Clean the pantry

In some houses, this might not be an area to worry about, but if you have some sort of pantry or a cupboard that holds your food, it is a good idea to clean it out. You might have to separate this into a few different categories of cleaning since this is a large job to handle. First, go through and take all the items from the shelves in the pantry. You might be surprised to find out how much of a mess is under all the food. Get some hot water and a clean cloth before cleaning off the tops of the shelves.

At this point, don't go through and just toss the food items back in pace. Instead, go through and organize the food to make it easier to find. Rather than spending extra time finding food or figuring out if you have enough of an item, you can organize the food to make it easier to find and get supper started. You can organize by the name of the food, by what kind of food item, or use the method that works for you.

If you have the time each week and are ambitious, some people will get some basic baskets and leave these in the pantry. They can then plan out the meals for each week and pace all the ingredients for each meal in each basket. When it is Monday, they reach into the Monday basket and make supper. This saves them time with meal planning during the day and since all the foods for one meal are in the same place, they are saving time as well.

Tip #8: Throw away old food

For this step, you can work on the pantry first and then move on to the fridge. As life gets busier and you have more things to work with, you might keep foods that are old or past their expiration dates inside your pantry and fridge. These are not healthy for your family and often they just take up space and add more clutter to the kitchen.

First, go through the pantry. As you are putting foods back in their proper face, take a look at the expiration dates on each box and can. If the food is past the date, throw it out right away to keep your family safe. You may want to consider doing the same thing with foods that are close to their date unless you have a plan to use this food within the next few days. This can clear up a lot of room in your pantry and can make grocery shopping easier.

Once you are done with the pantry, you can move on to the fridge. Do the same thing with this area. Look at the expiration dates and throw out anything that is old. Consider the sniff test as well; take a sniff of the food item and if it smell off, throw it out. This can clear out the fridge and ensure that the food you are serving your family will stay safe.

Tip #9: Take a look at the fridge

While you are on the fridge, you should consider cleaning it out. This can be really relaxing as a new mother, but make sure to start this process at the beginning of nap time so you have enough time in the day. First, take out all the food and throw away all of the items that are past their due date. Keep the food items out for a bit.

Now you can work on cleaning the fridge up a bit. If the shelves and drawers in your fridge come out, take them out and clean up inside a sink full of hot and soapy water. This helps to get rid of all the food that is getting nasty and not looking good on the shelves. Even if the shelves don't come out of your fridge, just a cloth with hot water will work as well.
Once the fridge is cleaned, you can move on to putting the food back in place. Try to organize the food as much as possible so you can find all the right items as soon as possible. You can organize by side, date to be used, or food type.

Tip #10: Sweep everyday and mop on occasion

Having debris on the floor of your kitchen can make it hard to keep clean. It is a good idea to sweep up the floor every night when you are done cooking supper. You can finish up the dishes and give the floor a nice sweep when done. This often takes just a few minutes if you keep up on the chore and can make the whole room look better.

While you don't need to do this every night, mopping once or twice a week can give the floor a nice shine. With kids, you always have things dropping and becoming sticky. A good mopping will get all this stuff off the floor and can make you feel so much better.

The kitchen often takes a lot of time to clean up. As a mother, you may not have time to sit down and do the work all at once. But separating this between a few days to start and then a little maintenance can make the process easier and with the help of these tips, your kitchen will look amazing in no time.

Clearing Out The Bathroom

By this point, you might be tired of cleaning the house. Being a mother can take all your energy and wear you out faster than anything else on the agenda. Adding in these decluttering projects, especially in the beginning, can really wear you out as well. But once you get the energy back a bit more, it's time to get working on the bathroom. As one of the hardest to clean and messiest rooms in the house, you may want to separate out the bathroom over a couple days to give it the full attention it deserves.

Tip #1: Medicine cabinet

Every home has a spot in their bathroom that holds all the essentials. Even if you don't take a lot of medications, this is the spot where diaper rash ointments, toothbrushes, toothpaste, shampoos, dental floss, tweezers, makeup, and Tylenol all end up in this area. While you might not have a specific spot in the bathroom that is a medicine cabinet, you might have a shelf or another place that holds these items.

The first step for helping out this part of the bathroom is to go through and see if the medication and items are up to date. If you no longer take the medication or an item has missed its expiration date, throw it out. You will be surprised that a lot of things you hold onto are just taking up space in the bathroom.

Next, get a few little storage bins that you can organize the different items. You might consider getting bins that separate things up like eye care, skin care, and hair products to make searching in the morning easier.

Tip #2: Keep things up high

Your new baby is soon going to be crawling and walking all over the place. The bathroom can be a really dangerous place for the baby if you leave things unattended. Go through all parts of the bathroom and take a look at what might cause danger to the baby. While you don't need to get rid of these items, you do need to take some precautions. For example, you still need that toilet bowel cleaner, but leaving it under the sink without child proof locks or right on the floor is just asking for your baby to take a drink of it. Figure out what your child might get into, and place it all up high out of reach.

Tip #3: Childproof the bathroom

This is an area where you need to really bring out the child proofing for your child. While this might not seem like part of your decluttering process, it will determine where you place items so they are out of reach of your child. Children like to get into things and it's easy to become distracted and miss out on something. When you take the time to child proof the bathroom, you are able to keep your baby safe.

First, work on the cabinets. If you plan to keep any cleaners, irons, or other harmful items under the sink counter, get a lock to place on the doors. There are several options available that keep your child out of the cupboards so you can still use them without worry. Next move on to the toilet. Children love to play in this easy to reach source of water, but falling in can be a big danger for little kids. Consider purchasing a child proof lock that will keep your child out of the toilet.

Tip #4: Hair control

As a woman, you are used to having hair products of all sorts and these products will get in the way when it comes to the bathroom. You might have different tools including hair holders, gels, sprays, curlers, combs, and hair dryers. These soon take over the whole bathroom counter and look like a mess. Adding in the different wires that can make tripping and falling a reality, and doing your hair can be dangerous.

Most people opt to purchase a big tub where all the hair items can go. You can throw them in when your hair is all done for the day and place the items under the sink or somewhere else that is easy to reach. When you need them the next morning, you just start the process again by taking out the tub. This keeps everything in one place while also keeping it all out of the way.

Tip #5: Towel storage

The first step is to get a towel rack. Most families will reuse a towel at least a few times before they clean it to save on laundry and time. But in most families, this one towel will get thrown on the floor when it's done being used. When four or five people do this, you end up with a pile of towels getting in the way. A towel rack can help with this problem because the towel is put out of the way and off the floor. If there are multiple people who use different towels each day, you can consider getting hooks. These go conveniently on the back of a door and each person can have their own.

Of course, a towel rack or the towel hooks are not going to be enough to hold on to every towel that you own. This means that you must use some creativity to get the towels put away. In some cases, using one of your cabinets will work for this option. Other times, getting a small little cabinet or table can work well to hold all the towels.

Tip #6: Makeup storage

As a new mother, you probably don't think that much about the makeup you are wearing, but at some point you may want to get out of the house and stun people by how amazing you look. Plus you have all that makeup lying around from before the baby. Letting the makeup lie around the bathroom is just making it look crowded and unorganized, but when you put the items away, it becomes even harder to find them.

One good idea is to take a drawer in the bathroom and turn it into a makeup drawer. To do this, go out and purchase some small containers that will hold each individual items. You will need one for lipsticks, eye shadows, bush, and foundation and so on. Now place these inside the drawer. The next time you are ready to go out and have some fun, pull out this drawer and have all your makeup in one area.

Tip #7: Clean up the bathroom.

It seems likes a lot of clutter items end up on the floor of your bathroom. If you are in a hurry and just have a few minutes before the children attack, the best thing you can do for the bathroom is just clean it up a bit. To start, go through and grab up all the trash. You might want to keep a trash bag on hand to help clean up faster. Next, fill up the laundry basket with all the towels and clothes that get left behind on the floor. At this point, don't separate out what is clean and what is dirty; assume that all the clothing items are the floor are dirty and need to be taken care of. While you are at it, pick up the toys and return to the bedroom they belong.

Once the clutter on the floor is done, do a quick wipe down of the rest of the room. You can clean off the mirror and do a bit of the counter. With enough time, you might find that wiping down the toilet and the bathtub while sweeping the floor can give the appearance of the bathroom looking clean. Save the deep cleaning for later and just give a quick run through of the bathroom to make it feel better.

Tip #8: The shower caddy

In many bathrooms, you are going to be limited on the amount of space available, especially when it comes to your shower area. This means that a shower caddy might be the perfect option for you. This allows all your shower and bath time items to be in one place without scurrying around and trying to find things at the last minute.

The type of shower caddy that you use will depend on your area. Some people will have a nice corner unit that can hold a lot of items while others might use one that goes around the shower head. If you have the room, you might want to consider two. One will hold your shower items and the other will hold the items that your child uses. This puts everything into one place at the same time.

Once you have chosen the shower caddy you would like to use, go through and add the needed items. Do not add a lot of extra things as room is limited. On occasion, go through and throw out all the items that you no longer use, are empty, or are old. This keeps the shower caddy clean and lets you get more done in the bathroom.

Tip #9: Use the toilet

Most people don't take the time to realize that there is a lot of room that is just sitting empty above their toilet. They see the toilet and assume nothing can go in this area. But when you are dealing with a small bathroom and you need to store your items as well as your children's items, you need to use all the space that you have.

The area above the toilet is the perfect option. There are a lot of shelves and cabinets that can fit nicely over your toilet. Now you have an extra place to hold all the items you need and your bathroom is the same size as before.

Tip #10: Decorate with function

Decorating in the bathroom can be tough. You may want to put up something that is pretty and looks nice, but you are also limited on room. But when you turn your decorations into something that can also be used in that space, it becomes easier to get what you want.

There are a lot of ways that you can do this. For example, instead of using a regular towel rack, you can use one that has some nice color or decoration on the end. Some people will find colored jars and leave their hairpins, rubber bands, cotton balls, and other items there to keep them out of the way. With a little bit of creativity, you can make the bathroom look great without taking up space.

The bathroom is a difficult room to organize. There are many items that stay inside this room and need to be organized, but often it is easier to just throw them all over the place. With some of these great tips, you can get that bathroom organized during nap time and get on with other important duties.

Making Your Room a Clean Sleep Haven

Your bedroom is supposed to be a place of comfort and relaxation. This is the place you go when it's time to escape from the work of the day to get some sleep. A new baby can drain out the energy and by the end of the day you may just fall on the bed and hope to get some well needed rest. But when your room is a mess, it has been shown that you aren't getting the quality of sleep that you deserve. With these easy tips you can get your room cleaned up in no time and love the new amount of sleep you can enjoy.

Tip #1: Work on the bed.

If you just have a few minutes to clean up a bedroom, you should concentrate on the bed. This is where you sleep, but also the area where lots of things get thrown all over. No mother likes to spend all day trying to keep up with a baby just to come to their room and see a mess they must clean up on the bed before going to sleep. So just by concentrating on this part of the room, you can make a big difference.

To start, clear out all the clothes that are on the bed. Throw them into the laundry room or inside your laundry basket to deal with later. Any books or magazines that are in the way should go on a shelf or into your study or you should deal with them right away. Once the clutter is off the bed, the room will already look better.

Next is the bedding. At this time, you probably don't remember the next time that you cleaned off the sheets and the comforter; it was probably at least before the baby. Take these all off and throw them with the other clothes into the laundry room. Place some new sheets and a new comforter on the bed and make it nice and tight. While you don't need to replace the bedding each morning, at least keep these as fresh as possible and make the bed after each use. These steps just take a few minutes and can give the room a clean and airy feeling.

Tip #2: Invest in a laundry basket

It can save you a lot of time and effort having a laundry basket in your room. Many people change in their rooms and without the proper receptacle, they end up throwing these clothes all over the floor and making a mess. Find a nice little laundry basket that can fit into the closet and throw all your clothes inside rather than on the floor. Once the laundry basket is filled up, take it to the laundry room and do a load while there. This can keep the floor and other objects of your bedroom looking nicer and will also save you time making trips back and forth to the laundry room.

Tip #3: Get a shoe organizer

As a mother, you must wear a million hats during the day. You have to be a mother, a daycare provider, a worker, a cook, and a maid among your many titles. While wearing all these hats, you also have to have the shoes to match. But all these shoes can easily get in the way of a clean and organized bedroom. You will often just throw them wherever they land and if they are in the bedroom rather than all over the house, you have made some progress. But once nighttime comes and you trip and fall over your many shoes, you may realize that something needs to be done.

A shoe organizer is the best way to get these shoes off the floor and organized. There are a few different options that cover anywhere from four pairs of shoes to twenty and more. A good idea is to get a shoe caddy that can go on the back of your closet or bedroom door. This space isn't really being used anyway so might as well place your shoes there to keep them out of the way while saving space.

Tip #4: Clear out the clutter

Another task that should only take you a few minutes if you plan out the time right is to clear out the cutter that is in the bedroom. Just like with your bed, there is probably a lot of junk that is accumulating all over the room like on the floor, on your dresser, and on the shelves. You can clear up the room pretty quickly with just a bit of tidying up.

First, start out with cleaning up the floor. Any clothes that haven't made it to a laundry basket yet need to get there. You can pick up under the bed, on the floor, and refold the clothes that got messed up in the dresser so they fit nicer. Go find a trash bag to pick up any of the trash or items that are just in the way. If you eat in the bedroom, get those dishes out. Wipe down all surfaces as you go.

Next, work a bit on the dresser and your end table. When you are in a hurry with all your tasks, it is normal to throw things all over the place, including the surfaces of your bedroom. Take a bit of time and get these cleaned up to look nicer and give the room a better feel.

Tip #5: Invest in Totes

When it comes to your bedroom, you are going to be a bit limited on the space that you can use. But one area that is not utilized all that much is under the bed. This does not mean you should throw clothes and blankets under the bed and hope nobody notices the mess. The best way to do this process is to invest in some thin totes that will fit under the bed and look nice.

You can use these totes for any items that are needed at a later date, like blankets, winter coats, and outfits for the next season. While you are not using these right now, you will have a use for them later. But until that time, you need to keep the items out of the way to give the room a clean look. Just fill up the totes and place them under the bed for easy access.

Tip #6: Clean out the closet

Cleaning out the closet often takes the most time out of your bedroom cleaning experience. You may want to consider doing this on a day when your husband or other family member has time o watch your child so you can devote your whole attention to this task. To start, bring all of your clothes, shoes, purses, and other items out of the closet. If your bed has been cleaned off by this time, you can lay the items out since you will clean it all up.

First, let's look at the shoes. Place these in he shoe rack you already purchased to get them out of the way. Consider whether each pair fits or if you plan to ever wear he shoes again. If the answer is no o these questions, throw them out or donate them. It doesn't matter if you have room for the shoes in your shoe rack, get rid of them anyway. Do the same thing with the purses; if you can't remember the last time you used a particular purse, it is time to throw it out. You may not even need a purse for now since you're using the diaper bag for everything. Place the purses on a hanger to keep them out of the way.

Now it's on to the clothes. Take a look at all the clothes and figure out if you will wear them. You probably have a lot of maternity clothes in the closet; consider placing these in the totes under your bed or in storage in case you need them again, but get them out of the way. Next, figure out if you pan on ever wearing the clothes again. If you didn't fit in the outfit before your baby and haven' worn the outfit in years, you should just get rid of them.

By the time you go through this process, you have probably emptied out the closet a bit. Place he leftover clothes back into the closet and organize how you wish. Consider donating the other clothes to those in need.

Tip #7: Use the top of the closet

In most closets, there are shelves and other space available that most people don't use. While you shouldn't shove important things up in this area since it's hard to see, you can still use this space to keep organized. This is a good spot to store blankets, sheets, and other items that you need, but which aren't needed all the time.

Tip #8: Consider shelving

Shelving can be a nice addition even in the bedroom. In most cases, a small bookcase with a few shelves will be enough to do the job. This can be nice to hold the books that you read before bed, some of the baby items you keep in your room, or anything else of value. You can keep these out of the way and organized to make it easier to find.

If you are short on space in your bedroom, consider a nice corner shelf. This can give you two shelving areas in one spot. You can shove the shelf in the corner where it's out of the way and easier to use.

Tip # 9: Organize the nightstand

A nightstand is a great idea to have in your room if you have the room. This is a place to keep a glass of water at night, a book, glasses, or anything else that you need to keep close at night. Take some time to organize this area at least once a week. Items will often get caught up on the nightstand and will make the room look messy if you don't keep up with it all. Take the glass of water back to your kitchen, put the book back on the shelf, and store the glasses somewhere else to keep the room clean.

Even if you are short on room in your bedroom, you can still keep a nightstand. Just make sure to get a nightstand that can work as more than one thing. Rather than getting a small table to place by the bed, get one that has a drawer and a little shelf underneath. Now you have three different things in one and the nightstand doesn't take up as much space as before.

Tip #10: Get a smaller bed

Most couples have a bed that is bigger than what they need. While a big bed might seem like a nice idea, it can take up a lot of room in the bedroom and gives the room an appearance of being too small. Most couples don't need a California King bed, unless your husband is a professional football player. Going down to a queen bed, which is plenty for most couples, can offer you a lot of extra room without depriving you of a good night's sleep.

If you do plan to get a new bed, consider getting one that can work for more than one thing. There are some bed frames that can have little shelves in the bottom and a headstand that works like shelving. These are all attached to the bed and don't take up more room than the bed does. This allows you to organize the room without taking up more space.

Your bedroom should be a relaxing area that you can sit back and get some good sleep. Don't let a little clutter get in the way of feeling your best and getting ready for another busy day with a new baby.

Cleaning Up the Babies Room

The room that gets the biggest mess in the whole home is the baby room. Even if the baby doesn't spend much time in this room, lots of items end up collecting here. You leave the baby crib, the toys, diapers, and other paraphernalia in this room and just one time of baby playing in this room can make it a mess. Here are some of the tips you should follow to get this room cleaned up and looking its best.

Tip #1: Organize the clothes

Organizing a dresser for a baby can be difficult. You want to make sure the clothes are all in order so that they are easier to find while remaining wrinkle free and clean. It can be almost impossible for the first few years because the clothes are small, and you will go through them so many times a day.

A better option for younger children's clothes is to hang them up. You can organize by season, color or put all the pants and then the shirts together in one area. It helps to keep the clothes looking clean for as long as possible. You will also save time by being able just to glance in the closet and pick out the outfit you want rather than scrambling through the dresser. It may take a few more minutes during laundry day, but the amount of time you save later is well worth it.

While you are doing this process, take some time to see which clothes still fit. Your child is going to grow faster than you can believe in those first few months, and you may be amazed to find out how many of their clothes no longer fit. Go through and see which outfits you can get rid of and which ones can stay in the closet. For those that don't fit, either store the items for another baby if you plan to have more or donate them to someone in need. Once you have completed that project, you might notice the closet is empty. Now you may have to go shopping to get your child some new clothes to wear, but at least you have a good idea of what items are needed to save you time and money.

Tip #2: Have a place for bath stuff

Searching around for all the stuff you need for a baby can be a pain. You can waste a lot of time scrambling around trying to find these items, and you may even give up on the bath if you feel too tired. But when things are all organized in one place, you can get the bath done and baby off to bed in no time.

Instead of searching around for all your items, put them in one spot. You can pick a spot on the shelf for all the bath stuff and make sure you place every item back in place. To make things even easier, consider getting a bathroom caddy just for the baby. You can place all of the items inside the caddy and just grab it and go when bath time arrives. Just make sure that you renew any item that is running low so baby can have the best bath every time.

Tip #3: Have a place for changing stuff

Searching for diapers in the middle of the night, or even when you're tired during the day, can give you a headache. Putting all the items in the same place can solve this issue and get things back on track.

There are a few different methods you can make include either using a shelf or having a changing table. Some parents will choose the shelf because they like to have all items in one place or may not like taking up space for a changing table. You can place all the items for diaper changing time in the same place and come back to them whenever you need.

Many parents choose a changing table. It provides you a safe place to put the baby plus lots of drawers and shelves to put all the materials. As long as you keep the table stocked, you never have to go more than a few inches to grab any item you need to make diaper changing easy and painless.

Tip #4: Separate the toys

Even when the baby is first born, you are going to have a lot of different toys for your baby. Some of them may be age appropriate and, others might have been well-meaning friends and family who gave you toys for later. No matter the reason for having some of the toys, you need a place to store them and to keep them organized rather than letting them be all over the house.

The first thing you need to do is separate out the toys. Go through and fill up a small basket of toys that are age appropriate for your child and you would like to keep in the room. Find another box and fill it up with the rest of the toys. The toys in the basket are the ones your child can play with for now. The other box can go into the storage room or the top of your child's closet.

This is going to save you a lot of time and hassle and make your life easier. When the child gets tired of the first bunch of toys, you can switch them out with some of the toys in the big box. Plus you get some of the toys out of the way so, you have less to clean up each day.

Tip #5: Diaper genie is your friend

As a new parent, you should consider getting a diaper genie for your child's room. There are a ton of diapers you need to change throughout the day to keep your baby clean and happy. When it comes to getting rid of these diapers, you may run out of hands when carrying the baby, feeding them, and bringing toys out to the living room. Unless you gain some extra arms, you may leave the diaper in the room and forget about it until it's too late.

Instead of letting this happen, consider getting a diaper genie or another trash can in the room. Now when you are done with the diaper changing, you can throw the diaper inside and keep it off the floor and out of the way. Make sure to take the time to clean out the trash can as often as possible to keep the diapers from getting smelly.

Tip #6: Get a toy box early

When it comes to toys in your kids' room, you need to have a place to keep the toys. You may get the toys under control for a bit, but when well-meaning relatives come to visit you will have more toys than before. A nice toy box can help to make things easier for storage. While you might not put much in it for the first bit, you'll be surprised at how quickly the toys can build up and will be thankful for having the one-stop box to place them in.

Be careful when picking out the right toy box for your baby. There are a lot of varieties available. While the wooden and antique ones might look nice, you may want to consider going with something plastic instead. As your child begins to walk, it is more likely they can fall and get injured while they are moving around. A nice plastic one is nicer when it comes to fall, easy to clean for those pencil and crayon marks, and can take a beating a bit easier. Fisher-Price and StepOne options are great and you can easily pass them down to grandchildren or other children in your life.

Tip #7: Use the wall space

In every room you declutter, make good use of the wall space. You only get so much room on the floor and most parents think they are out of luck once they use that up. But many forget that the walls can be used to make things easier. Your walls are not just for your picture frames or for some of the decorations you choose for the room. Rather, you can use them up to make life easier.

First, consider getting some hanging shelves. These can look nice in the room without taking up more room on the floor. You can get a small one that holds bedtime stories, one for some toys, and one for the bathroom supplies. If you are pumping, you can consider getting a few hooks to leave the pump up off the floor but still in easy access to use. Anything that you can get up off the floor and away from the baby can make things so much easier.

Tip #8: Rocking Chair

Having a rocking chair in your baby room can be a great idea. Many children like to be rocked to sleep and you might not stand a chance of getting a break all day without one. But you should be smart about the rocking chair you choose. Instead of picking out the old-fashioned wooden rocking chair, pick out one that is going to make organization easier and still fit nicely in the baby room.

A rocking chair that works well is one that comes with an ottoman. Many of these will have an ottoman that can also work as a storage unit. You can place toys, blankets, or other necessities inside. Place the lid on top and your feet also have a nice place to relax while you are rocking the baby to sleep.

Tip #9: Keep some towels on hand

With a new baby, you never know when a mess is possible. It is a good idea to keep a few towels on hand in their room for all the messes. You can also consider some cleaning supplies to make things easier as long as you keep these supplies out of reach from your baby. Once you see a mess, clean it up right away. These items don't need to take up a lot of space; if you get the travel-sized options, it is possible to leave these on one of the shelves or even on a changing table. This can save time from running around the home trying to find the supplies before the stain sets into the furniture or carpet.

Tip #10: Sanitize the room

When your baby is young, it is easier for them to get sick. Whether it is flu season or not, it is a good idea to keep the room cleaned and free of germs. One way to do this is for you to stay away from those who are sick and prevent others who are sick from coming into your home. But since you can't keep all the germs away, you need to keep their room as clean as possible. As a new mother, cleaning on your hands and knees all afternoon is not a possibility, but if you use some sanitation methods, you can kill off a lot of germs without wasting all day long. Consider getting some sanitation wipes and going along all the things that your baby might touch or put in their mouth. While this is not enough to completely avoid the cleaning process, you can spend five minutes on this each day and keep your baby safe.

Keeping the baby room clean can be a challenge. The tips above can be done all at once or split up over a few days in order to get the work done. With a little bit of organization and hard work, you can make this room look spectacular.

Fixing the Closet

This might be a really small area in your home, but it is important when you want to keep things organized and have more room for storage. In many homes, the closet becomes the odd place to throw items without worrying about them until the closet door is no longer able to close. Here are some of the best tips that you can use in order to declutter your closet and make it easier to use for the things you really need.

Tip #1: Empty out the closet

The first thing you need to do is empty out the closet. You are wasting a lot of time cleaning out a closet if you haven't taken everything out yet. Things will get thrown behind other items and soon you are missing out on a lot of junk and staring at a closet that isn't getting any cleaner. Whether you have one storage closet or ten in your house, take the time to bring everything out of each one.

Find a designated spot in your home where you can place all of the items. A guest room or a little corner of the living or dining room can be nice. This allows you the opportunity to come back to the work if it takes too long without placing the items back inside and losing your place. Take everything out so the closet is completely empty. The rest of your objective will be to put as few things back into the closet as possible.

Tip #2: Get rid of what doesn't fit

In most cases, you might choose to work on the closet because things are not fitting as well as before. You may not be able to close the door because the item is too big. The best option is to get rid of all the items that don't fit. Take a look at these objects. Are they not fitting into the closet because you are out of room or because they are too big? If the items aren't fitting in because you are out of room, wait a bit until you can sort through some of the other objects and see if there is room later on. This is the most common reason an item isn't fitting into the closet and after you finish, you might be surprised at how much room is leftover.

In some cases, you might find that the item is just too big to fit into the limited space of the closet, even when the closet is cleaned out. Now it is time to make a decision. If the item is something important or you plan to use it later, such as a holiday decoration, you may want to bring it to the storage room. If it's just taking up space and is broken, ruined, or you have no use for it, it is now time to throw it out and make more room in your home.

Tip #3: Get some hangers

There will be many items in your storage closets that can be hung up rather than thrown down on the floor. This throwing method can make the floor and the whole closet look messy and cluttered. When you hang things up, you will be able to free up the space on the floor to hold other items and make it easier to find the items that you are looking for. Purchase these in bulk because you probably have more items than you imagine and you can use any extras for your bedroom closet.

While you are hanging up items, take a look to see if you should keep the item or not. If you have some baby coats that your child no longer fits into, you can consider donating them to someone in need or store them in case you have more children. You may still have that high school letterman's coat for your husband or that one coat you bought at the store hoping to lose weight, but now is the time to get rid of them. These are just taking up space and once you lose the baby weight, you can reward yourself with a new coat or wardrobe.

Tip #4: Do a vacuum clean

While the closet is still cleared out, take the time to vacuum the carpet. If you have linoleum flooring, you can sweep and mop the floor. Over time, the floor is going to become disgusting with all those boxes and other items sitting on top of this. If you want to keep the room clean, it is time to do the vacuuming. Remember through this decluttering process that you need to try to keep as much of the floor open and clear as possible. Once the floor starts to get covered up, you have the issue of too much stuff in the small area.

Tip #5: Replace the light bulb

Short on time and want to make sure that you can have the storage closet looking better than before, consider changing out the light bulb so that it is brighter and easier to see. How many times have you scrambled around in the closet hoping to find something? You probably waste a lot of time trying to find the missing object and either find it a long time later or give up in frustration. With a brand new light bulb in place, you will be able to see around the closet easier and find all the items you need. When the closet is clean and a new light bulb in place, you will never have trouble again.

When picking out a light bulb go with one that is really bright and can last for a long time. There are some energy efficient models available that can really help out with making the light brighter. These can also save on your utility bill and they last longer than other bulbs you can purchase. If your storage closet doesn't have any light source, you need to consider putting one in to help out.

Tip #6: Throw out anything that is broken

There are a ton of things you have thrown into your storage closet over time. You may have thrown a few things in here that are broken or something else may have broken after some time in the closet. When you see these items take a moment to look them over and determine if you will ever fix that item. In most cases, you will not want to spend the money to fix it or it's beyond repair. Don't waste any more time or space with these items and just throw them out.

If you end up needing that item again, you can go out and purchase them again. While it might be tempting to save money with the broken items by saving them and fixing them up, it is not likely that you will actually do this. Plus it often costs more money to repair an item than it does to purchase a new one. So open up the space in your storage closet and see which items you can get rid of.

Tip #7: Get a hanging rack

While you can hang up a lot of clothes on the regular rack in the closet, you may have some other items that need special attention. You can purchase the hanging rack that works for your needs. If you need to keep some swimsuits out of the way you can get a hanging rack. Ties can go on this area as well as necklaces and anything else you are keeping out of the way. Consider getting a little hanging rack tree to hold on to your scarves and hats for those winter months rather than trying to dig through the closet or a box when the weather finally starts to cool down for winter.

Tip #8: Organize by season

There are different seasons that your clothing will follow. You have the warm stuff for the summer, the cooler stuff for fall and spring and something really heavy and comfy for those cold winter months. When it comes to the storage closet, there might not be as much variety but you still have some seasons present. Why not organize things by the season you would wear them, especially when it comes to your bedroom closet. This might take a bit of time, but you can go through and find the items easily the next time you need them. No more sifting through clothes, coats, and other items; you can just take a look at them and grab what you need in two seconds.

As you are doing this process, take the time to figure out which items you will keep and which you will give or throw away. This can be a hard process to do. After having a baby, it is difficult to fit back into your old clothes again, even if you lose all the weight. You may want to consider donating all the clothes you used to wear after baby and investing in some new clothes that fit your new body and make you feel good. Take the time to box up your maternity clothes as well since you might not need these for a bit. Take what's left and organize by season to make the closet clean and easy to use.

Tip #9: Consider small shelves

Depending on the size of your storage closet, you may want to get some small shelves to place inside. This gives you more room than before to store things and can add a bit of organization to the whole space. You can figure out the shelves that work out the best for your own needs. Some people will just place one little shelf in the back of the closet to separate out boxes and others will get a bit more elaborate.

There are a few ideas that you can do with this shelving idea. You can place the one in the back like discussed above. Some people may put shelving all around the walls of your storage closet to make things easier and to add a ton of space as well. If you can find some sturdy hanging shelves you may place them on the back of the door. The size, amount, and length of your shelving will vary depending on the amount of space in the storage closet as well as what you plan to do with the room.

Tip #10: Use the back of the door

Just like with some of the other rooms you are working on, you should make good use of the back of your storage closet door. This space is just sitting there waiting to be used without taking up the floor or the hanger space inside. There are a few options that you can use here to make the back door efficient. Using a shoe caddy on the back door can be nice whether you want to hold some of your extra pairs of shoes or you need a nice place to hold your mittens and scarves. You can hook up some little containers on the back of the door to hold odds and ends that have no other home in your house. Get a few hooks to put on the door to hold up some necklaces or a tie holder. Be creative and you will find a ton of ideas that use this space while keeping things off the floor.

The storage closet can easily become a place that catches all the random items in your home. Often you will throw something there without even thinking. Months later, the items are still piling up and you really have no use for them. With a little bit of organization you can get rid of these items and have a nice and clean storage closet.

Picking Up the Toys

As a new parent, you are sure to have toys going all over the place. Your child will leave them in each room of the house and often you will trip over them in the middle of the night. While you are not able to completely get rid of the toys or get them out of your way all the time, you can take a few precautions to keep as many toys out of the way and also help keep the cleaning process simpler than before. Here are a few ideas that you can use in order to declutter your home when the toys seem to be taking over.

Tip #1: Keep the toys to a minimum

The first tip that you can do is minimize the number of toys. It is tempting as a new parent to purchase every toy that you see to keep your baby busy. Your family will tell you how great a toy is or how much easier life will be with this and that toy and those advertising make it seem like life is not complete without another item for your baby. But most children are happy with just a few toys at a time and all the other ones will just end up in the way.

So if you're tired of having toys all over the place, consider getting rid of them. You can donate these toys to someone in need or give them to a neighbor kid. Your child, even if you have more than one, is not going to need a million toys all over the place and getting rid of them in this way can help to reduce your mess while doing a good service for someone else. In the future, refrain from purchasing more toys that will get in the way.

Each time someone gives you a new toy for the child or if you want to purchase a new toy, such as during a birthday or Christmas, consider getting rid of some new toys. By this time your baby may have outgrown some of the toys that they already use. If you are worried about too many toys coming into your home, consider asking relatives for books for the child to learn how to read, movie tickets to their favorite new show, or another idea that brings about a new experience rather than more toys.

Tip #2: Consider separating out the toys

Kids sometimes get bored with the toys they are playing with. After time, something doesn't seem as exciting as it did in the past. When a new toy comes into existence, or at least one they haven't seen in some time, the excitement can come back. With this tip, you can use this excitement to your advantage to clean up some of the toys while reducing the amount that you need to purchase.

With this idea, go through all the toys that your child has. Split them up in two. You can have your own method for splitting them up, but it doesn't matter that much. With one half, put them back in the toy box or wherever they belong in your organizational pattern. With the other half, you will box them up and place them in the basement. Allow your child to play with the first batch for a couple of months. When they get a bit bored with the toys, you can switch them out and bring up the second batch. Not only have you cleared up some of the mess lying about, but you have also brought some new excitement to your child even though they are using old toys.

Tip #3: Keep a storage container in each room where toys are present.

Toys are never going to just stay in your child's room, no matter how hard you try. Even though some of the other examples below will concentrate on ways to keep toys organized in your child's room, there are going to be plenty of times when your living room, bedroom, and even kitchen are overtaken by toys of all kinds. While cleaning up all these toys once they come out is an option, this can take up a lot of your free time and drive you insane.

Rather than wasting time when you are short on it and have other things to do, consider getting a couple small containers to leave around the house. You can get fancy and have a toy box or wooden box or just use a plastic container you have left over in your home. Leave these in high traffic areas, like the kitchen, to collect the toys. Next time you have a pile of toys in your living room, you can just throw them in the container and leave them for the next playtime. If these toys really drive you crazy, you can move them back to the child's room.

Tip #4: Label containers for use

Containers will become your best friend when you are trying to keep toys off the floor and out of your way. You should go out and purchase some containers that you like and will go with the décor in your child's room. Some people like to use little flower tins while others will go simpler and just pick some plastic boxes. You can place these things on a shelf or hang them on the wall, keeping in mind that you need to keep the containers at a reachable level for your child.

Once you have the containers picked out, take some time to label them. You can have one container for Lego's, one for cars, and so on until all the little toys are going to have their own spot. If your child is not able to read yet, print out some pictures of the items for each container to make things easier. All the big toys will probably go into the toy box so don't worry about that at this time. Show your child the containers and explain what goes into each one. Now your child is able to place the items away to help out and find the items they need when they are ready to play.

Tip #5: Use pencil bags for those random puzzle pieces

Puzzles are a great way for your child to learn new things and to figure out how to problem solve. But keeping track of all those puzzle pieces can be a hard task. You may try your hardest to place the pieces all back in their places, but one time of your child getting ahold of them and you are lost. Soon you will end up with random pieces to ten different puzzles and none of them will be complete.

A good idea to keep these puzzles in place is to use some pencil bags. You can get different colors for each puzzle. For all the small puzzles you will be using with your child, the pieces will fit into these pencil bags in no time. Zip them up and store them someplace safe until the next time you are ready to play. When you are done putting the puzzle together, you and your child can place all the pieces back in without worrying how they will stick together or not fall apart when putting them away.

Tip #6: Magnetic strips for cars

Over time, your child is going to collect a lot of cars to play with. Little boys love to have cars all over the place and collecting all of them can be a hassle at the end of the day. You may try to purchase a little container to place the cars in, but getting this filled up and making sure you have enough room in the container is a difficult process. Plus once your kid opens the lid of the container, the cars are going to end up all over the place.

Rather than going through this hassle, consider getting some magnetic strips and put them on the wall. While this might look a little bit strange on the wall, there is a purpose for keeping the cars out of the way. You can then place a little piece of magnet on each car so that they stick better to the strip; in some cases the cars will have the right magnets inside so you can just place them on the strip. The next time your child wants to play with just a few of the cars, they can reach up and get what they want without the mess or the hassle.

Tip #7: Trundle beds become storage

The trundle bed will become your best friend as your child gets older. Over time, they will no longer fit into their baby cribs and you need to find something that is a bit bigger to fit the growing boy or girl. But you need to be smart about the kind of bed you purchase for your child. Instead of picking out a regular bed, pick out one that is efficient and can do several purposes for picking up toys.

A trundle bed is a good option for you to get for your child. This is plenty big for a little toddler and you can pick out from a few different options. When picking out the trundle bed, go for one that has some storage inside of it. There are some that have drawers attached to the bottom of the frame. These allow you to place toys, blankets, clothes, and other options in the drawers. They are out of the way but still really easy for your child to grab whenever they are ready to play.

Tip #8: Use a shoe organizer to hold some toys

The shoe organizer is not just for the shoes that your child has. You can also place some toys inside. If you are able to hook these onto the door for easy access at a lower range for your child, you really have things set up. Get a sturdy one of plastic so that your child is able to see what toys are inside and your child will be able to reach in and go off to play. You just need to make sure that your child places the toy back inside the container when done.

There are a lot of things that you can place inside the shoe organizer to keep things together. If your child is into action figures, these fit nicely into the shoe organizer and they can just grab one before running off to play. Cars can fit nicely in here as well as some of the bigger Lego's that are hard on the feet when you fall on them. Barbie dolls fit well in here as well. You can put any extra toys that are hanging around and that your kids play with often to keep the room clean and organized. Plus with the shoe organizer right on the door, you will be able to have your kids put the items away quickly as well.

Tip #9: Pasta jars for the small toys and crafts

Doing crafts can be a fun way for your child to learn and grow but when it comes to all the items you need for these crafts, things can become messy. Rather than throwing out the materials that you are using because you don't have room somewhere else, you can take the crafts and place them into some pasta jars. This is a great option if you have lots of buttons, glitter, cotton balls, Popsicle sticks and so much more. Your child will be able to see right into the jar and pick out what they need to make a beautiful collage or other project.

You can go about this in a few different ways. The first is to be really creative and make the jars look even more fun. You can go out and pick out some jars that are different colors. It is pretty easy to find some jars that are red, green, yellow, and blue. You can place all the crafts inside so that they look nice. If you are trying to save some money, you can just use some of the pasta jars that you use in the pantry and fill these up. These might not be as pretty inside, but they will be easier to look inside the jar and find the item that you need.

Tip #10: Use a wood bottle crate to hold the cars

As your little boy grows, they are going to become interested in cars and soon you have a million little metal cars all over your floor. Instead of leaving these and other small toys all over the place, you can consider bringing out a wood bottle crate. You can use this just as it is or you can paint it up to make it look better for the décor. When it is time for bed, have your child place their cars and small items inside to keep them out of the way. Your child will love that the wood bottle crate will look like a little garage for their cars and is easy to reach and you will love having a cleaner room and home.

Keeping the toys off the floor and out of your way is one of the biggest challenges you will face as a new mother. Use some of the tips above to get your home back in order and to make it easier for your child to still play.

Cleaning Up the Storage Room

The storage room is an area of the house that is the most forgotten. You probably only go down there to throw some item or another inside and then go looking for something you cannot find. This often leaves the room a big mess and over time you may quit going to the storage room because of the mess and because you can't find anything inside. While you are working on your decluttering projects, it is a good idea to spend a bit of time on the storage room. This is a big room though and there are lots of little things to do, so consider splitting it up between a few days. Here are some of the tips you can follow in order to clean up the storage room and make it easier to find the things you need.

Tip #1: Get some sturdy shelving

Leaving boxes and other items on the floor is never a good idea in the storage room. First, this brings up the risk of you staking boxes too high and then they come toppling down. Second, if some water ends up in the basement, your boxes could get wet and soggy and depending on the items inside, you may lose some of your valuable possessions.

A good way to solve this issue is to get some sturdy shelving. You do have some freedom in choices here, just remember you will probably put some heavy boxes on top these shelves so pick something that can hold some weight. There are some nice plastic shelves available that won't rust and will keep the items safe or you can go with some of the more old-fashioned metal options as well.

After you are done organizing the whole storage room, remember to put the boxes back on the shelves. This will keep the boxes and their items safe until you need them later. Remember on occasion to remove the items and clean off the shelves to keep them nice.

Tip #2: Get some big plastic boxes

Storing things safely is important when it comes to your storage room. This is the area where you keep a lot of valuable items as well as those you would like to use later but don't have room for at this time. One mistake that people make with their storage rooms is using regular cardboard boxes. While these may be sturdy and can hold a lot of different items, they are not always the best choice.

Think of this situation. One day you get a big rainstorm in your area that just won't go away. You end up getting some flooding and of course it all goes right down to the basement. Your boxes get wet and the water starts to seep in towards the contents inside the boxes. Now some of your favorite memories are ruined because the water came in and the boxes weren't strong enough.

For storage room use, big plastic boxes will work the best. You can find these all over the place and with some shopping especially at garage sales you can find some of these for a good price. Go through the storage room and consider how many boxes you will need to complete this project. You can then fill them up, put a label on top, and store the items safely. The next time that some rain or water gets into the storage-room you can rest assured that your valuable items remain safe.

Tip #3: Keep everything visible

When picking out your boxes, you may want to consider getting some that are clear. You will still want to pick the ones that are sturdy plastics, but see through can make your life so much easier. While many people like to get the sturdy plastic ones that are colored and you can't see through, these can make searching through things hard. You aren't able to just look through the box to figure out what's inside. Even putting a label on top can leave you guessing, especially if the label happens to fall off.

Picking out see through boxes can make things so much easier. Before digging through the box and trying to figure out what's inside, you can just glance at it and have a good idea. This saves you time searching through the storage area plus will keep the mess at bay. Although you can see most of the items inside, you may want to consider putting a label on these boxes as well. This can save you even more time.

Tip #4: Sort out the clothes

Clothes are one item that you will place in the storage room. You could have winter clothes down there during the summer, some of the clothes you fit in before you had the baby, and even old children's clothes that you are saving for your next child. Over time, these clothes become mashed up and hard to separate out and you will have a big mess on your hands. This is why you need to spend some time sorting out your clothes.

Since this is a big job, you may want to consider asking your husband to help bring the clothes upstairs so you can work on them while your child plays. Your goal with this is to reduce down the clothes to just the ones you need and throw out everything else. Once that is done, organization is going to take some time as well so having the boxes upstairs can make it easier to work and watch baby.

With the exception of baby clothes if you plan to have another one, your job is to weed out the clothes you have. First, look at the baby clothes. Are there some that are really dirty and worn down? Would you want to receive these as gifts from someone else or have your own baby wear them again? You might find that some are really dirty or miss-colored from use so dump these out. You can fold up the rest nicely and put them in one of the see through containers to save for your next one. If you aren't planning on having more kids, the job becomes easier. Organize the clothes by the age of the child and find a friend or nonprofit group to donate these clothes to help out someone in need.

Now that the baby clothes are done, it's time to move on to the adult clothes. Unless you aren't planning on having another baby, find all the maternity clothes and put them together in one box. You probably have a small little box of these since the pregnancy was only for a few months so this shouldn't take long. If you don't plan to have more children, get rid of them to someone in need. Next, go to the clothes you kept from before the baby. Are you actually going to be able to fit into these again? Are these still in good shape? Remember that even if you lose the weight, your body is different now than before baby so you may not fit in your old clothes. It might be a better idea to give these away and purchase some new clothes as a reward for your hard work.

Once that is done, go through all of your other clothes. Look and see which ones are worn out, too big or small, or that you never plan to wear again. Throw all of these away. By this point your giving away pile is probably really large, but this will save so much room inside your storage room. Once you have just a few clothes left, pack up the boxes and label before enlisting help again to bring the boxes back downstairs.

Tip #5: Throw out anything old and broken

Just like your upstairs closets, the storage room is full of items you threw in to get out of the way. This can include almost anything and getting it all cleaned up is a pain. While you may have thought you'd come down for an item at some point, it most likely stayed there long past that date and was forgotten until you found it now.

When it comes to items in the storage room, you should throw out any item that is broken, ripped or old. If it has been in the storage room for some time, you have managed life just fine without it and throwing the item out is the easiest thing to do. Unless the item ripped or broken is an old family heirloom or like a quilt from your great grandmother, there is really no reason to worry about fixing the item. In most cases, you would just leave the item in the storage room or have it lying around the rest of the house and this item would never get fixed. Save yourself the time, hassle, and space and just throw it all out.

Tip #6: Clean off the shelves and the cobwebs

Each time you go down to the storage room to clean up, make sure that you clean off all the shelving. If you have just put the shelving in, this isn't as big of a deal, but you may still want to rub them down with a bit of cleaning solution to get them ready for later. But with older shelves, you may need to give them a bit of attention and care.

Get ready to give your arms a good workout for this process. It probably has been a while since you came down to the storage room which means the cobwebs and dust have had plenty of time to grow. Find some cleaning solution that has antibacterial properties and that can give off a nice smell in your storage room. Now scrub and get the shelving back to normal and looking brand new.

It is usually best to do this right after you get the items from the shelves. This allows the cleaning solution time to dry before you put the boxes back up to store. You can work on your organizing project and have clear and dry shelving when you're done.

Tip #7: Organize by holidays

There are a few different ways that you can organize your storage room and the method you use is all up to you. One good method is to sort by the holidays. Many of the items that end up in a storage room are holiday items like decorations for Christmas, Halloween, and Thanksgiving and so on. Once the items are placed in the box you will use, consider organizing based on this method. It is not a good idea to place all holiday items in one box. This is just asking for a mess as you sort through all the items just to get one holiday. Give each one its own box and then place the boxes in order on the shelves.

Once the holiday items are on the shelves, you can begin to sort out some of the other boxes in the room. Clothes are a good second so organize based on the weather, such as summer, winter, and fall. You can also have a shelf for the maternity clothes so that you can wear them when the next baby comes along.

One thing you should remember is to place a label on all the boxes. Even if you chose boxes that are easy to see through, put a label on top of the box. This makes it easier to figure out what is in each one and you won't have to search around as long when you are finally in need of these items.

Tip #8: Give back what you borrowed

The storage room will collect a lot of dust and items that you haven't used for a long time. While the whole purchase of this room is to keep things organized and store them until they are needed again, this doesn't always happen. Since the storage room is out of the way, you will often forget that an item is down there. Soon all the items collect and you don't even know what is in the room.

While you are sorting things out, you will begin to notice some items that don't belong to you. These are often items that someone lent out to you at some point and for which you forgot to return. Do not hold on to these items; they are only taking up space in your storage room and if you have forgotten for this long that you had an item that didn't belong to you, you are not likely to use it again in the near future.

Now you have two choices. If you know whom this item belongs to, give it back to them as soon as possible. They may have forgotten about it too by this point but they will be happy to get it back. If you have no idea who the item belongs to, it is time to donate to someone in need. Obviously the original owner has not been bugging you to get the item back since you don't remember it so you might as well give it to someone else. The choice is up to you just don't keep it in the basement any longer.

Tip #9: Make a little play area for tornadoes

Many people in America will understand how horrible tornadoes can be. These can be even worse for a new mother who must get their child to the basement while watching the weather and keeping everyone calm. While this is not a fun situation for anyone involved, there are a few steps that you can take to make the situation better and more comfortable.

To make your child feel a bit better about the confusing situation, consider creating a little play area. You can keep some of the toys that you are hiding, some blankets, and some drinks to keep your child calm. You can even pick out some music to play, perhaps some of their favorite songs, so they can sing and dance along while you worry about the weather. Your child might be so excited about all the lost toys they find in this area that they won't notice all the commotion and bad weather going on above them.

Each of these areas is going to be different for every parent. Think of all the things that your child would enjoy when they are scared or to get them to sit still for an extended period of time. If your child is a newborn, consider keeping some water and formula down in this play area so you can feed them when they get upset. Snacks for older kids and some drinks can be nice as well. Keeping your kids happy and calm is important during an emergency and you should plan out some of these things out and get the items ahead of time while decluttering your storage room.

Tip #10: Keep a spot for hidden toys

As mentioned in the previous chapter, it is a good idea to keep some toys saved away to help keep your child interested without having to purchase more toys over time. When you are cleaning out the storage room, take some time to clear out a space to put some of these toys. You probably don't need much room for this, but make sure that you have room for one or two boxes worth.

There are a few things that you should keep in mind about this hiding place. First, the place needs to be somewhat hidden in case your child goes down into the basement on any regularity. This will prevent your child from seeing the toys and wanting to play with them or bring them back up before the scheduled time. Another thing to keep in mind is to place the toys in a place you can easily access. You don't want to create a mess in the storage room just to bring out a few toys.

The storage room might not be an area you spend a lot of time in, but it still deserves a little bit of your time. This is an area where you need to keep a lot of items, like holiday decorations, winter clothes, and some tools, for when you need them later. But organizing this room can be almost impossible without some determination and easy decluttering tips. Get that room organized in no time and make it easier to find the things you need when you use these helpful tips.

Keeping the Diaper Bag Cleaned and Ready to Go

The diaper bag is another important part of your day that you need to take good care of. This bag is your new lifeline; wherever you and the baby go, this bag will go as well. Often mothers are in such a hurry that they grab the bag, or forget it at home, and it doesn't hold all the essentials needed. This can make for a long trip just going to the grocery store. Here are some tips on how to keep your diaper bag clean and make sure it's ready to go when you are.

Tip #1: Pack the diapers

The first thing you should never forget is diapers. Before even heading out the door take a look through your diaper bag and ensure that you have a few of these inside. The second you leave your home without these important items, you are asking for trouble. Leave at least three or four in the bag in case the situation gets really messy or you are gone for longer than planned. Even if you forget everything else that is recommended below, having diapers around can make the trip bearable when things go wrong.

Tip #2: Travel sized diaper wipes

Once the diapers are packed, make sure to pack up some diaper wipes that are travel sized so they can fit in the corner and are out of the way. You can purchase some of these in the grocery store and just keep replenishing when you run out. These are easier than using some paper towels or other material while at the store and they won't take up as much room as your traditional diaper wipe.

Some people may choose to purchase a travel sized diaper wipe container and then will just refill it with their own diaper wipes when it runs out to save some money.

You can also make some of these on your old. Take some of your regular diaper wipes and fold them up to be a bit smaller. Place sure that you put them inside a plastic bag or some other material that will keep them clean and fresh. Whichever way you choose to use, make sure to replenish the diaper wipes once they are done.

Tip #3: Clean out the diaper bag

Not only do you need to ensure that you are keeping the diaper bag stocked with all the necessary items, but you do need to clean it out on occasion. You would be amazed at how many times a bottle will dump over, some food gets stuck in there, or some other mess is made inside the diaper bag. Leaving this inside will just make the bag smell bad and you might not be able to use it.

Cleaning out the diaper bag does not have to be as complicated as it sounds. You can simply find a nice washcloth and clean it out as soon as a mess is made. If you are low on time and not able to clean it out as often as you would like, consider washing it in the laundry. You will need to read the washing instructions on your particular bag, but most of them will work out just fine with your regular laundry. This can make the bag nice and fresh and you can be on your way in no time.

Tip #4: Keep somewhere easy to find

If you are like most mothers, you have spent a lot of time looking around for the diaper bag. You will swear that you left it in one area but after ten minutes of looking you are getting frustrated that this item keeps disappearing. You need to make a place in your home where the diaper bag goes and it doesn't move until you head out the door again.

This doesn't mean you should just throw the bag on the floor when you get home. Rather, you need a designated space that keeps it out of the way. If you already have a coat rack in your home, consider placing the diaper bag there. You can then throw the bag up on these hooks the second you get home and grab it on your way out the door. If you have a place in your home where you like to use the items in the diaper bag or where you check that al the items are inside, keep the diaper bag inside. Just place a nice little hook on the wall in the room you want it and hanging the bag up as soon as possible.

Tip #5: Keep some formula inside

It is a good idea to keep a bit of formula inside the diaper bag each time that you get out. Even if you are breastfeeding, keeping a little bit of travel-sized formula inside can make a big difference. For the breastfeeding mothers, there are going to be times when breastfeeding is difficult. If you are on a long drive and there isn't anywhere safe to pull over, stopping to breastfeed can be difficult. Your baby might feel nervous at a specific location and not want to latch on and having the formula can be helpful. While you might not use the formula that often, it can make things easier in a pinch and give you a bit of a break.

If you are really into breastfeeding and don't want to use the formula, consider getting a little cooler pack for the diaper bag. You can then take along a few extra ounces of breast milk just in case your baby needs it and also keep the milk cold.

For those mothers who use formula, keep a bit on hand. A few packets might be a good idea in case you are gone for a long amount of time. You never know when a baby is going to get hungry and listening to them scream for twenty minutes or more can break any mother's heart. When the formula is there, you can just go find some water, or bring your own, and get a bottle made in just a few minutes.

Tip #6: Extra pair of clothes

Before you head out of the house, make sure to pack up at least an extra pair of pants for your baby. You may want to do a few pairs of whole clothes. Anyone who has been a parent can tell you a horror story about going out to grab some milk and having a messy diaper get all over their child's outfit and getting everywhere. For the expert parents, it is possible to just reach into the diaper bag and pull out a new outfit. Those new parents may have had to go out and grab a new outfit from the racks to get their child cleaned up.

To avoid getting a big mess and almost ending up in tears, which is likely to occur if you forget, you should bring along an extra outfit or two for your child. This way when you get a bad diaper or have a mess from spit up or other issues, you can reach into the diaper bag and change their outfit. Try to get at least a pair of pants, although spit up is just as common as other messes so a whole outfit or two is even better.

Tip #7: Age appropriate toys for long trips

Long trips can be hard for a kid, but you must remember that a long trip to a kid can be five minutes to the grocery store. If you go away for a longer trip to visit family or for a shopping trip, you need to be prepared. Having some toys in the diaper bag can make things so much easier in the long term. Any time the child gets fussy, you can bring these out and make them laugh.

Be careful with the types of toys you are using. You need to find some that will work well in different situations. For example, choosing some of the chain links can be nice. These hook on to the car seat as well as the cart inside the store. Your child can use their imagination, chew on these links when their teeth hurt, and just have fun while you get the errands done. You can pick out the toys that work the best for your child, but keep in mind the amount of space in the diaper bag.

Tip #8: Extra cash

While you are most likely going to take your wallet along on each trip, there are times when you will forget this important item on the dining room table. Without some extra cash on hand, you may have just wasted time going to the store for milk and not being able to purchase it. This can be frustrating as a new parent and will often result in two trips, the original one and one back and forth, just to get a simple item.

You don't have to save a lot of money inside the diaper bag. Keeping a $20 inside can help to make things easier just in case you forget. Being a new mother, or having a couple little kids running around, can make it easy to forget. With this money inside the diaper bag, you are safe to get what is needed. Make sure to hide this money in a location that is harder to find so no one get ahold of it and replenish the money you use so it's there for the next time you are forgetful.

Tip #9: Socks and shoes

Socks and shoes seem to disappear all of the time. When winter comes along, it is easy to misplace these items and you won't want to go out without a pair of socks to keep your baby's feet warm. Even when you place these items on before leaving the house, it is common for them to fall off and disappear in the car, at the store, and everywhere in between. When you keep a couple of these items in the diaper bag, it is not as big of an issue when one disappears. You can just pull one out of the diaper bag and then get on with the errands.

It is best to keep at least a few pairs of socks in the diaper bag Baby's seem to be fluent in taking off socks and getting them lost and you may end up needing both pairs just for one trip. These are often enough to keep the feet warm when it's cold. A pair of shoes is nice as well if the baby loses theirs, but socks will often do the trick just fine.

Tip #10: Extra shirt for yourself

While we have already discussed the important of bringing extra clothes along for the baby, you should also consider bringing along an extra shirt for yourself. Not only will the baby make a mess all over themselves but they are able to get the mess all over you. In some cases, they may barely have a mess on themselves and it all ends up on top of you. Without an extra shirt in the diaper bag, you might have to spend the rest of the trip smelling like spit up and looking disgusting.

Pick out a shirt that you won't miss all that much but that is comfortable. A nice white one or something plain that will work for different occasions regardless of where you go and the mess arises. Once the baby makes this mess, you can just change over to the new shirt without a worry and still look amazing.

Tip #11: Extra bottles

Always pack along some extra bottles for the baby. You never know when one might go missing. Babies like to experiment with their world and a bottle could easily go missing when you are turned the other way. You may not notice that the bottle is gone until it's too late and you are stuck at the furthest point from getting any assistance.

You don't have to pick out a bottle that is big and takes up a lot of room. Many times your baby can be satisfied with a few ounces until you get home. Pick out a small bottle that fits in the corner of the diaper bag and keep it ready for use. You will be happy you did the next time those tears come up and you are scrambling around to find the bottle.

Tip #12: Extra pacifier

Pacifiers are your best friend when they are nearby and your baby is happy but can turn around and be your worst enemy when the pacifier is missing and your baby is screaming at the top of their lungs. And of course this always happens at the worst possible times; in the car in the middle of nowhere, in the middle of a meeting or church, or in the ones tore in town that doesn't sell the right type of pacifiers.

Instead of going through the baby tantrum and feeling like you should attempt one as well, consider placing one or two extra pacifiers inside your diaper bag. These are small and easy to keep out of the way. You can then offer one to your baby while you search around in peace for the other one. This saves you time and headaches and can make the outing so much better.

Keep this in mind with all of the important items that the baby enjoys. You can keep an extra blanket or an extra of their favorite cuddle toy inside. This can help to soothe them down when the errands run a bit long and you can't get out of the place quick enough. You can be the super mom with a well-behaved baby and your child will feel comforted and more willing to go along until you are done.

Keeping your baby happy and satisfied is the goal of the diaper bag. Make sure to keep it stocked with some of the tips listed above so that you and your baby can get the chores done without a big meltdown in the store.

Easy and Quick Decluttering Tips Before Company Comes Over

As a new mother, it is not likely you allow too many people over to your home. You are already busy with all the tasks that you have to keep up with during the day and with a new baby on your hands. It is not often that you have time to make the house presentable for company. But at times, company insists on coming over, you do have a cute new baby to take care of, and now you are stuck trying to make your home look presentable. Don't pull your hair out over this situation; here are some of the best decluttering tips that you can try out to get your home in shape before company comes over.

Tip #1: Start in the kitchen and bathroom

Sometimes you need to decide what the most important part of the home to clean up is. Unless your company has given you a few weeks notice, you can't get it all done and you may have to make some sacrifices in order to get the home to look nice. When you are really short on time, it is a good idea to pick a few rooms that you can make look amazing to impress your company. The first two rooms you should concentrate on are the kitchen and the bathroom.

Many new mothers will spend a lot of time in the living room. While this is a good place since people spend a lot of time in the living room visiting. But this room often takes just a few minutes to fix up and people will be happy. Plus you have the excuse of a new baby taking over the living room so this room doesn't have to look perfect.

First, start on the kitchen. This is a room that can easily get messy and your company will notice pretty quickly. Take some extra time to make the kitchen look as good as possible, even more than you do on your own.

Next, move on to the bathroom. This room can get messy and will look poorly on your house cleaning skills if it is a mess the whole time your family and friends are visiting. Not only is cleaning up the room nice, but adding in a few extra touches can make your family feel more invited. You can keep a few extra toothbrushes around in case they forget theirs at home. Keep some shampoos and lotions around as well. Make sure that the towels are all cleaned to make things easier and to really impress.

Tip #2: Get cleaning supplies ready

Before you go and clean the whole house, make sure to organize all the cleaning supplies that you plan to use for each room. You can actually waste a lot of time running back and forth to get the different supplies needed to keep the house clean. And when a baby is involved, you are already short on the time needed to clean the house. If you get everything prepared ahead of time and bring the items along with you to each room, it is much easier to keep moving and getting the area clean.

The best way to bring along all the supplies that you need is to find a little shower caddy or other container that is easy to move. Plan out what needs to be cleaned in each room and then what supplies are needed to get the job done. Place these cleaning items into the caddy before starting. Now you can bring the items to each room and keep moving without having to stop to find the items you missed.

Tip #3: Avoid the windows

One place that new mothers will spend too much time on when they are expecting company is the windows. Windows seem to take a long time to get done and you could spend your energy and frustrations on another part your guests are actually going to notice. Unless you have some time later on, leave the windows alone because they don't look that bad and your guests won't even notice whether the windows are sparkling or not.

If the windows are really bothering you, be a little selective about what you clean. You can pick the ones that are really bad, like the ones with a lot of little fingerprints. The windows can be important, but since most people aren't staring out your windows and noticing them while visiting, there are better uses for your time unless the windows are really dirty.

Tip #4: Do some dusting

Dusting is often the last thing you will do as a new mother. When it takes all day to keep the clothes and toys off the floor, it doesn't make sense to do a lot of dusting. But when company plans to come over, it is time to dust to make the house look better. Plus it can save you time on other occasions when you don't have as much time.

You don't have to make dusting a big deal. While it is possible to grab some Lysol and a few dish cloths to make the house smell nice, it is also possible to clean up the whole house when you're in a hurry. Some people find that getting a little Swiffer dust cloth or other similar item will work much better. You can hook this up and get through the whole house in just a few minutes without having to waste time or worry about the house having a strange smell.

Tip #5: Pick up the trash and clutter

No matter how short of notice someone gives you, go through and get as much of the trash and clutter that is in your way. This alone is going to make a big difference in the appearance of the house, even if you don't have all day to clean. You can do this in three different sweeps of the house. For the first sweep, grab a box and pick up all the dishes in every room of the home. Bring those to the kitchen so that you can wash them off or place in the dishwasher.

For the second sweep, bring a laundry basket. It doesn't matter how long ago you cleaned up the house, you are sure to find some clothes lying around on the floor. You can go through the whole home and pick up the clothes before taking them to your laundry room. If you have time, start up a load of laundry while you work on the rest of the house. For the third sweep, go through with a big trash bag and pick up anything that you want to get rid of. You may need to bring a few trash bags to keep up with the mess.

By this time, your home is going to look a lot better, and if you brought the right tools, you got all this cleaned up much faster than in the past. Make sure to do a quick sweep with the vacuum and already your home looks so much better.

Tip #6: Spend extra time on the guest room

If a guest is planning on staying over for a night or more, you should spend as much time as possible in the guest room and the bathroom they will be using. This is an area they are sleeping in and probably won't have any other distractions to keep them busy. This means the guests might notice any mistakes and messes in this room more than in one of the other rooms. Consider spending a bit of extra time in this room to make your guests feel welcome.

First, start with the bed. Wash and dry the sheets and if the weather is nice, leave the blankets out on the line to give them a fresh smell. Leave a few extra blankets in the closet or the dresser in case the guests get cold and maybe a few bottles of water so they don't need to stumble around in the middle of the night to get a drink. Make sure the pillows are in good order and don't smell bad. Even if you don't have a guest bedroom, you can take some extra time on whatever room in the home you are using for this purpose. Consider adding in a few special touches based on what your guests might like.

Take some time on the guest bathroom as well. Consider some of the items you enjoy when you go out visiting. Keep the shampoo and conditioner easy to access as well as some of your nicer towels and washcloths. You can even keep some extra toothbrushes and toothpaste available to make things easier on guests who may have forgotten some of their items.

Tip #7: Use the slow cooker

Depending on when company comes over, you may need to feed them something while visiting. Even if they aren't planning on eating with you, if their visit lasts longer, you need to feed your family. Rather than throwing something unhealthy into the slow cooker, going out to eat and wasting money, or being in the awkward position of not having anything to offer your guests, consider bringing out the slow cooker.

There are tons of recipes you can use in the slow cooker to please even the pickiest of guests. You can keep a few recipes on hand in case someone shows up unexpectedly. It takes just a few minutes to prepare the ingredients in most recipes and then you can get to the other cleaning projects while a tasty meal is being cooked. Now you can be the host that does it all by offering a warm meal without putting in any extra effort.

Tip #8: Vacuum

Sometimes when you are really short on time, a nice vacuum of the room can make a big difference. This allows you to pick up all the little things on the carpet and often can make the whole carpet and room smell better than before. If you are using this as your main point of cleaning, make sure that you get under and around all the items.

This is the perfect option to make the room look instantly better when you get that last minute phone call that someone is on their way right now. But you should also consider vacuuming even when you have a bit more time. Get as much of the room cleaned up before vacuuming so you can keep all the little bits of trash and food from the floor.

When the hall closet is vacuumed out, consider going through the rest of the hallway. This area shouldn't be too messy at this point unless you are storing some random objects there. Get all of the other objects out of the way they present a tripping and safety hazard to you and the baby, before getting it cleaned. The storage room can work nicely while your relatives are there and you can go through the items later if you are out of time now. Now take the time to clean up any cobwebs that may accumulate in these areas and do a thorough vacuuming to make the area feel better.

Tip #9: Have boxes ready to go

Sometimes company announces themselves with just a few hours to spare and you just can't get everything done. You may have to resort to some cheating to get this all to work out for you. Instead of shoving things into the closet, something that is sure to backfire the second a relative or friend tries to hang up their coat, you can keep a few boxes in your closet. These can be plastic or cardboard boxes as long as they will fit nicely into the shelf somewhere in the closet and will hold a lot of stuff.

When you are short on time before family comes to visit, grab anything you don't have time to sort out and throw them in these boxes. It doesn't matter how organized they are as long as you can keep the boxes able to close. Once a box is full, take it back to the closet, close it up, and place it out of the way. This might not be the more organized way to get things picked up, but it allows you to have a nice clean house before the relatives come over.

You will probably just need two or three of these boxes to make the house look nicer. And if you've done a good job cleaning out the hall closet, you will have plenty of room to put these new boxes. While this is a bit of a way to cheat when you're expecting company, it can reduce the stress you are feeling and still gets the house cleaned up.

Tip #10: Do what you can

While it is tempting to get everything in order so that the home looks perfect, you want to give off the appearance of being perfect and being able to keep up with the new baby as well as your house cleaning duties. But this isn't always a reality for most mothers. It always seems like the day you need to clean and get ready in the last moment, your little one needs more attention than normal. Just do what you can to get the work done before the company arrives. You are just one person and if you don't have anyone else around to help out, you can only get so much done during the day. Those who come to visit you will understand that you are busy and won't mind if the house is perfect.

Sometimes you can't do anything about having family and friends come over at the last minute; you do have the cute baby they all want to see. But with some of these great tips, you can get the house looking presentable so others are impressed by how hard you worked.

Cleaning Out the Vehicle

Getting things ready to go in your vehicle for a trip, whether it is short or long, can be difficult. You want to get out of the house as quickly as possible and with very little fuss, but babies need a lot of things. Here are some things that you can consider when you are packing up the vehicle to make sure you are prepared even when the day is not going as planned.

Tip #1: Keep a small trash bag in the car

Even before you brought home your baby, trash had a way of piling up inside your vehicle. And now that the baby has come home to live, the trash issue is going to become worse. Whether you have to change some dirty diapers in the car, have some cans of formula to dump out, or you have moved on to the snacking phase for your child, trash is going to end up everywhere.

Most parents leave this trash alone and assume they will clean it up later. This usually doesn't happen until the vehicle gets so messy that things fall out when you open the door and the task seems like too much work. One way to make this easier and to ensure your vehicle stays clean is to keep a small trash bag inside. Some people like to use a little plastic grocery bag. As soon as you are done using something, place it into the bag instead of throwing the item on the floor. Once the little grocery bag is filled up, dump it out and start with a new one.

Tip #2: Keep some extra diapers

While you should try to keep the diaper bag as full as possible with necessities, every mother has rushed out the door while forgetting something important. You may be able to make due without the extra bottle or that pair of clothes, going without a diaper is a horrible experience. Even if you packed enough diapers, the trip may last a bit too long and you will need another one. Unless you are at the grocery store or someplace close to a store, you might be out of luck. And since you are never in the right place at the right time, you and your poor child will suffer until you can get back home.

One way to prevent the issues of forgetfulness in motherhood is to keep a few extra diapers in your vehicle. You don't have to keep very many, just two or three just in case something comes up. You can just replenish the stash once you purchase a new pack of diapers or whenever your child goes up to a new size. This can keep you calm when that horrible moment of realization of the forgotten diapers dawns on you. Consider keeping a few diaper wipes there as well. All mothers forget things on occasion, but keeping a little stash of diapers and diaper wipes can help keep things under control.

Tip #3: Load up the stroller

No matter how long you are planning on being gone, even if it's just for a few minutes to go get milk, keep the stroller in the wagon. You never know when something might come up and you need to be gone for longer. Say the tire blows out in the van a few blocks from home. Now you can load up the baby and some of your groceries and walk home rather than waiting around for someone to show up. Say that the weather is nice for the first time in months and you decide to go on a quick walk. Now you won't have to go all the way back home and get the stroller but can just head out to enjoy the beautiful day. There are probably plenty of times you will not use the stroller even when it's in the back of your vehicle, but you will sure appreciate the extra effort for those times you do end up needing it.

Tip #4: Have a toy bin

Toys are going to become your new best friend when you are traveling around with a baby. Even going five minutes to the grocery store stuck inside the car seat can be torture to your child. Bringing along some toys to entertain them can help bring laughter rather than tears to the whole trip.

But over time, the toys are going to begin clogging up the car. Your child will learn to throw the items and you will just grab another one. Soon the whole floor is covered with toys and you are probably too tired to pick them up. Don't let the toys take over your car as well as all the other aspects of your home. Consider getting a nice toy bin. There are several varieties available and most will just hook onto the back of one of the front seats.

These toy bins are really nice. First, they allow you to place the toys inside once the trip is done. You will no longer have a mess all over the floor but your child can still play rather than getting bored. Having the toys in this bin can actually save you some hassle because you can just reach in and grab another one rather than having to entertain your child on your own or try to reach around to pick up any toy that was thrown. Finally, as your child gets older, they will be able to reach into the bin and pull out the toys they would like to play with on their own.

Tip #5: Invest in baby music songs

For babies, music is one of the best ways to keep them calm while also expanding their mental capacities. This is why you should invest in some baby music songs for your car. There are some great ones available and you can use them as your child gets older to include some learning options. These can be on longer than the TV because your child interacts with the songs more and won't cause any strain to their eyes.

Make this an educational part of the day. You can have the child sing along to the song or see if they are able to guess which words are coming up next in the song. You can also sing along with them in order to keep them engaged and active. While you may start dreaming about the songs on your child's favorite CD after hearing it twenty times, you will be amazed at how quickly the time goes by when your child is having fun.

Tip #6: For long trips, consider a small TV

The longer the trip you take the harder it will be to entertain your child. This is when a small car TV can come in handy. While this might not be the best idea for younger children because the TV will be close to their faces and they may not be able to concentrate inside the car, your older children may enjoy the TV.

When using this in the car, make sure you only have it on for a bit. Your child should not spend an 8-hour road trip watching TV the whole time. This is something to have on as an aid to give yourself a little reprieve and to make the trip go a bit faster. Choose one movie or show and let your child watch it before switching to another activity.

You should also try to find something that is a bit more educational for your child to watch. There are a ton of great options you can choose from to teach your child colors, letters, numbers, and sometimes even languages. Now you are ensuring that your child can learn while they thing they are getting a treat.

Tip #7: Pack along some books

Reading to your baby is a fun way to help pass the time. If you are going on a long trip, consider keeping a few books in the car. You can tell your little one a nice story while driving along so they stop squirming and yelling for a bit of time. Not only is your child having some fun, but they are learning at the same time so you are practically supermom.

When picking out books, pick some that are pretty sturdy. The books in the back seat of the car like to take a beating and you want these to last for some time. Go with some pictures as well. When you are tired of reading the same story ten times in a row, you can hand over the book to your child and let them explore the pictures and scenery in the story. Watch your child's mind grow as you get some peace and quiet on a trip.

Tip #8: Keep a few extra pairs of clothes

Keeping a few extra pairs of clothes in the care can make a big difference. If your child has an accident in the car and you forgot to bring something along in the diaper bag, you will now have some options. When the weather is turning cold, consider keeping an extra coat or some other warm clothes in the back so that you can switch them out to stay comfortable. Do the same in the spring so your child doesn't get overheated. You can even leave a swimsuit in the back to get ready for the pool at any time.

If it is wintertime, consider putting some other winter supplies in the car as well. Some boats, a snowsuit, coat, and even hats and mittens can be nice too. You never know when the weather can turn bad or when you may need to abandon your vehicle to stay safe, and this is not the time you want to remember that you forgot the warm stuff for your baby at home. Keep these things in the vehicle so that you and your baby can stay safe.

Tip #9: Keep some play shoes in the vehicle

As winter comes up, you will want to make sure you have plenty of shoes for your baby. While you may remember to put the shoes on, and at times even this is a challenge when you are in a hurry and frustrated with the searching process, the shoes may still get lost. Babies like to have their feet free and will quickly learn how to get all shoes off. When this happens, you may be at the mall trying to get errands done but not wanting to look like the bad parent who let their kid go out without any shoes on.

Rather than letting this happen, take the time to keep a pair of shoes in the car. They don't need to be the nicest shoes, just make sure they fit. The next time your child plays Houdini with their shoes, you have a backup and their little toes can stay warm.

Conclusion

Decluttering your home can be a big undertaking, especially when you have a new baby in the picture. You are already spread out pretty thin, but this doesn't mean that a clean home that is safe for the baby isn't important. Most mothers figure they need to sacrifice in one place or another; they either need to spend more time with their babies and ignore the housework and how messy the house is getting or they spend time cleaning and let their baby fend for themselves. With some quick and easy decluttering tips, you are able to get the whole home cleaned up in just a few minutes each day.

Finally, there is some hope in the tunnel for those who are looking to get their home clean while still taking care of their baby. If you are able to spend five or ten minutes each day during naptime, you are able to get a few of these simple tasks done and your house will begin to look amazing. Take a look through this guidebook and learn just how easy decluttering your home as a new mother can be.

Thank You

Dear Readers,

Thank you so much for buying my book. I have been gathering housekeeping hints and tips ever since my college days and I have found it to be one of the best ways to keep relationships alive even when years and miles keep us apart.

I am always looking for ways to improve so if you enjoyed this book or have suggestions to make it better, feel free to leave a review.

Again, thank you for your readership and have a happy home!

Bree

CPSIA information can be obtained at www.ICGtesting.com
Printed in the USA
LVOW10s1445190216

475864LV00017B/574/P

APR 2 9 2016